Sex Siren

TALES OF A
LATER DATER

DONNA ARP WEITZMAN

To my mother, Coy Lee, for whom I hold unending admiration and gratitude. She helped to etch the Rules of Life in my brain and taught me to never compromise my core, yet remain flexible to life's changes. Always one to see the funny side of life, she gave me the gift of humor. Loving and laughing with Dad for 69 years, upon his passing she admitted at 89 years old that there was likely another Prince Charming somewhere waiting for her!

To my special sister, Betty Jean Willbanks. I can never thank her enough for liberating me from dangerous mind games in relationships with her continuous message: "Others have power over me only if I grant them the privilege of power." Thank you, Betty Jean. Goodbye mind games!

Table of Contents

Introduction

With many sexless nights behind you, you may have assigned yourself the title "forever single." If your hopes for the perfect man no longer linger on the surface but instead harbor far below, this book is for you. If you spend your time reminiscing about the many errant arrows that Cupid has launched in your search for sexy prey, help is on the way. Within these pages are sure-fire secrets to fulfilling your fantasy of procuring your Prince.

~~~~~~~

> With many sexless nights behind you, you may have assigned yourself the title "forever single."

~~~~~~~

Or at least they'll give you a good laugh along the way.

It will take a little study of the secrets herein and several practice sessions, but securing a soul mate can indeed produce a sensible outcome. My first book, *Cinderella Has Cellulite and Other Musings of a Last Wife*, was a satire about women finding love and remarrying later in life. *Sex and the Siren: Tales of a Later Dater* presents comical situations common among later daters. After a divorce or the death of a spouse, Sirens feel suspended between worlds. Will we ever find love again? And if we do, what will it be like?

In today's culture it is accepted that women have power. It is also okay to use our power in the dating world. Single Sirens don't have to wait at home hoping for Prince Charming to drop in. They can search for their own love partner. Thus the question becomes, "Can we induce love?" The following satirical stories aim to explore the answer.

While it's definitely possible to become more sensitive to the male's divergent traits, it takes thorough research. Upon vigorous study you can approach the male species differently than the doofuses you dumped in the past. Sexy Sirens know that love can be induced through carefully crafted actions and convincing communication with your intended. Yes, soul sisters, some skepticism can be expected. But "nothing ventured, nothing gained" is sage advice to remember when you are home alone on Saturday nights. So forge ahead and forage the fields for fresh fellows! Prepare yourself like Marie Antoinette before a fete. Don't be foolish listening to the sad tales of your single sisters. Wisely make your own bed, and then let him lie in it.

Ponder precipitously the pointers you pick up in the following pages. Review whatever notes you have copiously concocted before you next open your door to the princely prey. Then the man you want will wilt before your alluring lair and be captivated by your newfound charms. He has little chance of slipping past you after these secrets have been instilled in his psyche.

Read on. Tonight you may be alone, but as a student of love, the odds tilt your way. Tomorrow can be tantalizing. Good luck, Siren!

Sex & the Siren

TALES OF A LATER DATER

Sirens and Sex

If your passport affirms a birthdate before the middle half of the last century (20th century that is), you are more than qualified to decide your own sexual behavior.

It is tempting to be coy about your state of singlehood, however you arrived at that status, be it widowhood, divorce, or just plain luck.

~~~~~~~~
It is tempting to be coy about your state of singlehood.
~~~~~~~~

Imagine, if you will, that ever since "Fred's" heart attack and his untimely passing, your standard line has been, "Fred was the only man for me. He was the first and will be the last." When your women's Bible study class of fellow single ladies inquires as to why you are still single, your supposedly sinless sisters may look at you with various states of belief. Some nod their pin-curled coifs in agreement, pursing their thin, straight lips while patting their freshly starched skirts. They agree Fred should be your last and that's that.

3

Others look at you in pity, mouths agape, and clear their throats uncomfortably. Monthly cut and color jobs are non-negotiable necessities for this kind. Avid participants on man-hunting trips to the Bingo games on Friday nights, they refuse to accept the theory that abstinence makes the heart grow fonder. They are fond of male company, especially if he pays for the dinner, and they're pretty proud of it too.

Gladys admires your dedication to becoming a later in life nun.

In particular, Gladys admires your dedication to becoming a later in life nun. But Betty Sue pities your lack of foresight. "How sad," she thinks. "My friend's sex life with Fred must have been baaad. A new man might put some spring back into her step! Maybe I'll invite her to Bingo this Friday."

In the meantime, resigned to your single status, you accept Gladys' invitation to a girls' night out. You're looking forward to another early dinner at Tony's Italian and getting some laughs at the new movie that everyone's recommending starring two of Hollywood's single women heroines, Meryl Streep and Diane Keaton. However, the universe has something else in mind for you tonight.

While you try to focus on your linguini and clams, your resolve to overlook the happy couple next to you popping another cork of Chianti is weakening. "Can he possibly be *that* funny?" you wonder as you notice the top button of the woman's silk top gaping open. Although arriving before you and your favorite spinsters, their Caesar salads appear untouched. How different the scene at Table 2 is from your night with Gladys and the Grandmas. Another story about the newest grandbaby is one story too much.

You make it through dinner only to once more have your thoughts stray as your waiter serves your slice of cheesecake. "I'm not that much over the hill," you ruminate, looking more closely at the oversexed duo next door. "I look at least as good as her. So why is she out on a date, and I'm not?"

How would you ever undress in front of anyone else?

Suddenly clouds appear, and your thoughts aren't so sunny. "How would you ever undress in front of anyone else?" another voice whispers in your mind. Knowing that just like an oak tree, a man could count your years by the folds on your thighs, your face starts getting red sitting at the table. How could a man want *you* when he might worry he could drown in the potholes medicinally termed as cellulite? You silently curse gravity for steadily transforming your firm B cups into merely another ripple on your torso. "No, I can never be like the mature naughty nymph at the next table," you tell yourself as you spoon in another bite of cheesecake. Besides, who needs that aggravation, right?

But when the lust-laden twosome bellows in laughter again, you suddenly remember a similar scene between you and Fred back in a day when gravity was still your friend. Four decades with a man in a same-sex marriage (meaning 40 years of sex the same old way) was an incentive for you to plan a sexy trip for two to Vegas. You specifically requested a room at a mirrors-on-the-ceiling hotel and were relieved that Sin City still offered this kind of sizzle.

You ordered the hot pink bikini panties from the Victoria's Secret catalog you knew he had hidden under the recliner cushion.

Thinking you would add some interest to your wardrobe and instill some excitement to Fred's life, you ordered the hot pink bikini panties from the Victoria's Secret catalog you knew he had hidden

under the recliner cushion. Though
mindful of his heart murmur, you felt fairly
secure, given he'd seen your troubled torso
enough times not to warrant a trip to the
desert's emergency facilities.

After checking in at the hotel, you
giggled to the bellman, "Can you bring
the bags right away?" in an attempt to
disguise the urgency of the moment. It was
imperative that you get into the bathroom
before Fred with your supplies to freshen up
and don your mail order purchase. When
you exited the bathroom and padded over
to the king size bed, Fred was ready for
sleep. He scolded you a bit for paying extra
for a bigger room. "Two double beds would
have been fine," he'd said, pooped from the
trip. However, he didn't feel up to the fight so
he let this one go.

Lowering the lights, and ignoring
Fred's bodily function sounds, you slipped
under the sheets and fondly locked eyes
with the girl Fred saw the first night 40
years ago. The image you see above you
in the reflection of the well-placed mirror
on the ceiling is not half bad! Wow, what
happened to you? Thanks to gravity, there

are no facial wrinkles, no dimpled thighs, no rolls of extra cholesterol—just smooth sailing for this belated beauty queen. Before you can peel your eyes away from this sight to behold, you realize Fred has slipped into slumber, ignoring the sublime sex kitten purring right next to him.

Disgusted by his lack of effort, you vowed never to forget what a mirrored ceiling can do for a woman, but not for a man. The mirror was no friend of Fred; it only amplified his back hair. "Fred got what he deserved," you think of the snoozing log beside you. Next time you need a little pick-me-up, you will just hold a hand mirror above you in your bedroom at home and save the extra money for cotton pjs.

However, the Vegas lesson on perfecting your imperfections has stayed with you all these years. And it's coming to mind tonight back at Tony's Italian. No longer listening to your friend opine about Grandbaby #5's swim lessons, you silently ponder your options. If a man ever took you home, you would not necessarily have to worry—especially if he were inebriated.

You've been thinking about remodeling the house with Fred's life insurance money anyway. You could have the handyman install a life-size mirror over your new mattress! You make quick mental preparations to always be on the bottom, regardless of the man's preferences. Afterward, you can ensure that he's sleeping on his back so that when he awakes the next morning and glances up, you will still be the tight and toned tart he so desires! Why not then welcome an abundance of overnight visitors? After all, you were voted Most Social in your high school senior class.

A sexy Siren is born.

As Table 2 anxiously signals for the check, you take a long look at your spinster sisters. You are not going to share your secrets. They will just have to wonder the next time they see you why you are smiling so much. "There's no reason I should be celibate," you assure yourself on your drive home that evening. And if the handyman is available next week to install a large ceiling mirror, you will be on your way to having the body to prove it.

Sink or Swim

As a newly minted Siren, you may still remember the sting of transitioning to singledom. You can be caught unaware by moments of sheer fright about how your life as you knew it fell away. Like many Sirens who go through divorce, your plight was terrifying and you felt tainted and taboo, ostracized and avoided at all costs.

Instead of reaching out and buoying your spirits, your so-called friends conveniently forgot your cell phone number.

Instead of reaching out and buoying your spirits, your so-called friends conveniently forgot your cell phone number. The unceasing caste system of marrieds vs. singles widened the divide between how they may have felt and how they acted. Your situation saddened them for so many reasons, mainly their own fears. Frightened that their own lives could vanish if their marriages fell apart, you suddenly reminded them of their potential for odious outcomes. A single Siren on the prowl is just too unpredictable for some. You can read their minds: "She's surely on the make and may try to steal my husband!" Little did you know how you could ignite such terror among your peers.

You soldiered on alone on numerous nights where your sole nutrition came from leftover pizza or maybe just a glass of cheap wine.

Suddenly single, you soldiered on alone on numerous nights where your sole nutrition came from leftover pizza, or a simple scoop of ice cream, or maybe just a glass of cheap wine. Your thoughts taunted your psyche with demon-like interrogations—what if this became your life for the next few decades or more?

However, that night with your girlfriends at Tony's served to remind yourself that you alone can determine your destiny and strengthened your resolve not to give up entirely. You remembered the several pairs of sexy stilettos, some glamour boots, and a few kitten heels in the back of your closet. Surely, you told yourself, they would be enough to ensure you were sufficiently shod in the singles arena. Your instincts were right.

Little did you know how you could ignite such terror among your peers.

The more self-sufficient you became in the coming days and weeks, the more men seemed to find you irresistible. To your astonishment, your newfound self-assurance appeared to serve as a drug to most guys, and your social life became a whirlwind. You text, swipe, and post like it's your job. Keep in mind, Sirens are up to date on Twitter, Snapchat, and all forms of communication. If an Internet mogul is in your future, you assume the sure way to lose his interest is to proudly exclaim, "Any man who wants to date me needs to call me. I don't do email."

~~~~~~~~

You accept each invitation and smile wider than usual when encountering the overly curious inquiries into your life.

~~~~~~~~

No longer always a onesie at events, your former friends, the stay-aways, took note as they stepped closer into their ever-present chat circle. "Have you seen her?" "She looks good." "She must have got a hefty divorce settlement." "The new man on her arm certainly looks better than the old one." "Maybe we should invite her to lunch and find out what's going on?"

Never a fool, you know what's about to happen. The wedded wenches will begin including you in second-tier lesser luncheons. The ones doing the inviting will cagily explain when other soul sisters question, "Why her?" "Well," they'll respond, "I just thought it would be nice to include her."

The ones doing the inviting will cagily explain when other soul sisters question, "Why her?"

You accept each invitation and smile wider than usual when encountering the overly curious inquiries into your life. You give only the information you choose to share and are certain to ask about their children. You never, ever inquire about their mates, as this could renew their waning suspicion. Remember, until hell freezes over or a band of gold encircles her finger, a single Siren is forever suspicious.

Although you've carved a new life for yourself apart from these women, your mother taught you to turn the other cheek. You enjoy your new single girlfriends and often have a good time with the men you choose to humor with your time. But these fair weather felines were heretofore in your friend circle, and it's never wise to fritter away old friendships.

Did He Ask How Old I Am?

You remember them. The days when your body parts stayed where God initially put them. Your boobs sat high and wide like Bob Seger famously described in a song. You didn't have to pull your saggy eyelids tight in order to apply eyeliner and your booty somewhat resembled a Kardashian's backside. Unless your address is 13 miles from the nearest rock on the second right turn past Nowhere and the post office long ago abandoned your domicile, you are forced to admit that our society celebrates youth and every perky, upturned piece of flesh—if only for a few calendar years.

But before securing your new sexy Siren self with a suggested surgeon, it is wise to revisit your past—jut one more trip down memory lane with every last moisturizer and buzzing medical device known to mankind. Having been called a realist most of your life, you admittedly began your search for the fountain of youth long ago. Half-empty bottles of promises bought at cosmetics counters and on late night television yielded little in the lustful pursuit of "smooth and lifted skin." You've had your cellulite ground down and your face shaved by a fancy sander. You've slathered on FDA-approved acids and smoothed your skin with salicylic sauce.

~~~~~~~

Half-empty bottles of promises bought at cosmetics counters and on late night television yielded little in the lustful pursuit of "smooth and lifted skin."

~~~~~~~

All to no avail.

A few girlfriends smugly declare themselves devoid of ego and have loudly denounced the prospect of plastic surgery. But really, you never believed those girls and always found it easy to joke about needing an overhaul and upcoming calendar dates with Dr. Look Good or at least Dr. Look Better. Now you're no longer joking.

You begin by cagily extracting the
names of skilled craftsmen from your
carefully controlled amigas. They answer
haltingly, explaining how their doctor
barely touched their beautiful bounty. Or,
once you've pierced their vow of silence,
they go into exhaustive detail regarding
swelling so bad as to have resembled
King Kong, bandages wound so tightly
they became claustrophobic for the first
time, and scars that made their wrinkles
appear tiny in comparison. "Wow," you
think, realizing this is an all or nothing
situation.

What if something goes wrong? Your
face may not like Dr. Don't Turn Back Now.
Your nose may really like the bump it has
had since birth. Your eyes may insist on
hoods, and your chin might spite you by
developing a sharp point like Cinderella's
ugly stepsister. Soft, sensual beauty might
be out of your realm of possibility. Or even
worse, what if your doc's allergies cause a
sneeze that takes off a mid-surgery slice of
your nasolabial fold in the wink of your no-
longer-hooded eye? At the wrong instant,
a single ill-timed cough could pierce
your eyelid and make for an emergency

ophthalmologist visit. After all, doctors are not all angels. Am I right?

Still, having considered all the options, it is you and you alone who should make the plastic surgery decision. Yes, you have girlfriends who have done it for their husbands and boyfriends. But not you. Not Miss Independence. Not the one woman who will not be manipulated by any man. This is for your peace of mind and happiness. You are the one who looks in the mirror.

Well, at least for now. However, your trusted girlfriend has told you about an interesting new man in Houston. He's successful, newly single, and quite a catch. You are excited. You've asked many questions about him, almost to the point of your girlfriend's exhaustion and irritation. Knowing he is passing through your town in a couple of months, your mind goes into overdrive. You realize there is still time to overhaul.

"Just one more question," you coyly inquire. "Did you tell him how old I am?"

The Louse is Married

I t is forgivable to most that you
mistakenly thought the devilishly good-
looking rogue hovering over the cold
cuts at the buffet was unattached. After all,
recent LASIK surgery had afforded you an
uninterrupted view of his fourth left finger
and alas you saw no gold shining in your
enhanced monovision.

"This might be worth the effort!" you'd
told yourself as you dabbed a small
cracker in your guacamole, suddenly
glad you'd shaved and washed your hair
for this shindig. You remember sidling
up to him to make your move as he
shoveled shellfish. Never one to forget
the strict rules from Mrs. Garlington's
School for Young Women, you apologized
for staring, making certain to inform
him you were looking at the crustacean
assemblage.

Your training took it from there as you
remembered to "be coy and not overly
aggressive."

He was responding quickly and
affirmatively, smiling and asking your
name. "What a start to a potential tryst,"

you recall thinking. Your mind had then started to wander, already imagining him opening the car door as you slid in for a night on the town. Just when he seemed to be leaning in, ready to engage in the next level of conversation, you felt a precise jab in the ribs. It was your girlfriend, the hostess of the evening festivities. "He's married," she'd hissed. Your heart sank, another one having bit the dust.

The dumbest thing a new divorcée could do is to get involved with a married man.

It's a sick feeling you know so very well. "The dumbest thing a new divorcée could do is to get involved with a married man," you always tell yourself. Both your head and your gut know that playing with fire is never good. And dallying with a married man is surefire hell! Sure, some of your gal pals have borrowed husbands. Early on, they say it is fun and exciting... that's until the cat's out of the bag! Then

the complications in this sinister game
magnify exponentially.

During a married lover's early
onslaught of romance, a Siren can expect
roses—often two dozen, fresh from her
illicit lover. If the love fest lasts more
than a few turned pages on your desk
organizer, you can also expect diamonds.
Usually they're not big ones, as this
womanizer has to pay for everything
in cash, and securing enough cash for
several carats might make him a target for
the Fed and the Patriot Act.

Changing your calendar will
become commonplace to
accommodate Casanova.

This louse is the one who grabs his
cell phone and slips away from earshot
while you are waiting in the airlines club
for your next flight to Cabo. He sets up a
separate ringtone for each conquest. He
is a sly devil with a high IQ and smooth

lips. He often extols your virtues and is quick to make sure you know you are the only woman who has ever made him feel this way.

Keep in mind, Sirens, that if this is your type of guy, you will want to make sure of a few things. One, be certain you have spare lonely girlfriends who want an escort on Saturday nights, as you will need their company when your betrothed is with his betrothed at the bar mitzvah. Although his trickster ways have yielded him nights of ecstasy, his Saturday nights are reserved for the ball and chain! Second, also be aware that his homebound princess must never question his activities but be available to him on a moment's notice.

Changing your calendar will become commonplace to accommodate Casanova. And complaining can be considered catty—whether kitten or cougar. Siren, you can do better.

Competition with Kittens

D ating may be an open-trade system, but you need to know your enemies and learn to identify the threats. You know who she is—the young feline on the prowl for old and fat tomcats! She is enemy number one, dear Sirens. This delectable little dish has honed her hunting skills and her dewclaws. She learned at a very young age that there is little to profit by hanging around the male up-and-comers. This seductive sexpot is fully aware that the fastest way to maintain her fetching flesh is to find a CEO we'll call Mr. Schmuck.

Mr. Schmuck is likely a widower who has lost his long-time companion and best friend. After 50 years of marriage, he may even resemble his perished princess in certain lights. This man is like a freshly opened can of tuna for this baby cat. Schooled in the art of seduction while having another Grey Goose, she's spent countless hours with her cluster of captivating cronies. These ravaging renegades have taught her all their tricks. By now she knows that if you speak in a kittenish coo to the newly solitary single at the bar, he will welcome the warmth of your newly mink-wrapped body as he whisks you to the Hamptons.

～～～～～

"Well," she sighs, "getting him in bed was not a problem. But getting the ring was a bitch!"

～～～～～

If her prey is a recent divorcée, her safari is not as simple. She can only secretly hope that his last betrothed dumped him for her toned trainer. This man, she knows, is a madman on a mission. He'll want to show his jilting Jezebel that he can find a supple-fleshed female who will also make his buddies salivate on their six-packs of Bud Light. He wants a woman with a true heart but tight thighs, having convinced himself that he too is such a catch. "Hunting will be a snap," he thinks, not realizing that the hunter is soon to be the hunted.

A bit of a challenge for the masterful Madonna, she sets a different trap for this one. You overhear her schooling the hungry litter at their Wednesday night pub party afterward. "Well," she sighs, "getting him in bed was not a problem. But getting the ring was a bitch!" Her alluring femme fatales snicker as they dream of their big catch one day. The comely cosmetician vows, "Never will I have to clip another overgrown cuticle on some dude." Even you marvel at the depth of skill from the purring princess.

The very thought of being in the ring with all these perfected prizefighters causes a heinous headache.

That said, a Siren's most evil competitor on the dating scene may be the silly little machine sitting on your paramour's nightstand. Yes, the veritable tablet. When your pitiful prince does not pick up the check after yet another night on the town, it could be that his monthly obligations are not due to Little Johnny needing new shoes. It is more likely he has unyielding membership fees on any number of online dating sites. His red-rimmed eyes are not due to working late on his work project, as he says, but more likely to his late night perusing of the latest entries in his webbed world.

~~~~~~~~

You'd really like to meet an attainable alley cat of your own, you think, ignoring the younger kitties scampering underfoot.

~~~~~~~~

What's a Siren to do? The very thought of being in the ring with all these perfected prizefighters causes a heinous headache. Your mind runs rampant remembering the last time you sat at a lonely bar awaiting your aging coterie of singles to join you for a drink. You'd really like to meet an attainable alley cat of your own, you think, ignoring the younger kitties scampering underfoot. "If you see one, pussyfoot over to him and lick his ear," you hear them purring to each other. "It'll just be a few seconds before he will putty."

The only good news, you tell yourself, is that you no longer have to bother with pulling up your pantyhose, and you're free to don your bifocals because you are suddenly invisible to any XY chromosomes panting after these furry babies at the bar. You watch disgusted as you witness the chicanery of these chickadees. They are skilled, and they're bagging the buggers by the pawful.

Pulling out your phone to delete the names of the next six hot spot bars scribbled in your electronic organizer, you decide not to subject yourself to witnessing any more of this trickery. You are better than this. Just when you gather your purse to go home, there is a sudden deep stirring in your psyche. You find yourself sitting more erect on your barstool. You push out your drooping double Ds, having recently enhanced them if only to allow your bellybutton fresh air. Angling your designer-clad ankles toward the intended prey, you pull out your Estée Lauder purse spray and point it toward your expensive décolletage.

Yes, you are back in the game. Why is that? Because you are experienced. No mortal man can decline a determined Siren's advances. You know the piddly little pussies will soon tire of being pawed by the Social Security recipients. When his hands tremble and his AARP card falls out of his wallet while paying for the next martini, the little hussies will fade. Besides, you understand men like him. After all, you practically raised your last husband and learned to deal with his mother who firmly clutched her son from your wedding day to your second child's baby shower.

~~~~~~

Amateurs can go home if a Siren is sparring.

~~~~~~

You, Siren, you know exactly what works. You muster your courage and sidle up to the sought-after senior idling among the felines at the bar. You say something sensual. Not sexy, for even he is not that foolish. Then you slide away to sink into a chair slightly away from his sight. Then you wait, sipping your vodka martini and swinging your Jimmy Choos. Looking at you, any sensible soul mate will know he might have just crossed paths with a real woman of substance with spirited esprit de corps. This, he tells himself, is a woman who could ease his inadequacies and soothe his insecurities, while providing enough sizzle without his overdosing on Viagra.

Siren, you have prevailed as a proven female warrior. Amateurs can go home if a Siren is sparring. Your man-prey is now your man partner. As the two of you make plans for an early dinner and a movie next Saturday, happy mews turn into sullen hissing. "How did the old lady get that guy?" they question their clowder. As you lithely pass the litter, like a cunning coyote you offer the slight smile of the victor.

Siren Holiday Attire

Whether the Siren sails into Capri, flies into Rio, or drives up Highway 1 with her new man, she must have the appropriate appearance in order to keep her escort entertained. A Siren is fully aware that a successful respite on the Riviera can catapult her relationship's status.

For your potential trousseau, a critical item is your swimsuit cover-up. Many would-be Sirens think the lingerie is the deal sealer. Wrong! Remember, men are either hungry, horny, or sleepy, regardless of their marital status or fitness level.

> For your potential trousseau, a critical item is your swimsuit cover-up.

So what happens to your new La Perlas you have blown a fortune on before the trip? Luckily, they are either removed when he is aroused or they are ignored while he snores. But what happens when he is in his third state of being? He orders drinks and appetizers at the pool. This is the very time you want to appear appetizing.

What is necessary, but not hyper important, are the pretty little panties and a bra that covers back fat. Most Sirens know that it's what he can't see and only has an illusion of that keeps your travel mate enticed. If you, dear Siren, spend time and energy finding just the perfect poolside pieces of shimmering chiffon, he will have nary a wince when he sees you perched beside the pool. His mind will instead float back to the *Sports Illustrated* pin up of Farah Fawcett in a red swimsuit on his dorm room wall decades ago. Regardless of your hair color, he will likewise envision your blonde cascading mane falling over his chest when he has you in the picture-perfect position later.

Keep in mind that discretion is paramount when the sea breeze is whisking the silk around your ankles. The less flesh he sees, the better it will be for you. If your soul mate must ogle undimpled thighs, make sure he eyes only married women whose husbands issue menacing scowls at the slightest smile from your roving Romeo. You might gently tease him, smiling and remarking how these beauties' male protectors must spend hours pumping iron.

Remember, men are either hungry, horny, or sleepy, regardless of their marital status or fitness level.

Once satisfied with your gilded garment, you can now get on with packing for your upcoming love tryst. It is unnecessary to waste valuable minutes on your slacks, unless they could be mistaken for elastic-waisted parachute pants. Leave those at home. Even if you need to shed a few inches off your torso, slim fitting and carefully altered trousers are sufficient.

Selecting the silk to adorn your décolleté is far more important than whatever you're wearing on the bottom. Sitting on deck or at the small corner table in a faraway café, a carefully chosen caftan or low cut chemise can alter his appetite in a hurry. Whether you have the arms of Michelle Obama or they look more like slabs of pork shoulder ready for carving, you must consider your appendages at all times. Long sleeves can be sexy, and sleeveless can be tasteless if you have wrinkled skin, unsightly freckles, or cavernous pits in your upper arms. It is far better to wear three-quarter sleeves and a few charming bangles to keep your Prince Charming paying the tab.

An exposed bustline can explode your bliss. Breasts that resemble pendulous masses of untamed flesh should be hoisted, even if it takes a crane otherwise known as a full support bra. Never let nipples do a face off with your belly. Nipples must go up for air and not be pressed to the navel. Upon self-assessing with an unjaundiced eye, select your tops to wake up his animal, not scare him into the forest. Don't fool yourself; any extra weight you possess is not "all in the boobs." Mother Nature tends to be democratic, spreading it throughout your silhouette.

One last tip for when you are in the hotel room. Make-up should be hidden with only the tiniest stash exposed. You want your man to believe you have the natural beauty he remembers from his high school sweetheart days. Don't allow him to take note of your eye shadow and identify the streaks of color that has spilled on his side of the washbasin. No man wants to see an arsenal of beauty enhancements taking over the dressing table.

A Purse or a Nurse - Not Me!

A Siren who is widowed often gets emails from decades-long married girlfriends who know "just the right man." Let's name this perfect potential paramour Sam. Sam's wife died a few years ago and his designated mourning period has long since ended.

He's stable. This one is not about to mortgage his paid-off cottage for a red Corvette anytime soon.

They extoll Sam's virtues in detailed diatribes. This is a man of class. You won't see him in bars trying to entice young kittens to his pad. He is more prone to offer a chair to ladies your age. You've seen him in the country club, smiling and nodding to the widows, often stopping to ask about their grandchildren. "Isn't this just the kind of man you want?" your friends inquire. He's stable. This one is not about to mortgage his paid-off cottage for a red Corvette anytime soon. They convince you he simply wants a companion that can share his political views and snuggle.

~~~~~~

He starts his day counting pills prescribed for his numerous ailments.

~~~~~~

Yes, Siren, I said snuggle. You're no fool. You see past your friends' hard sell and realize that this is the kind of chap who would rather have you rub mentholated cream on his chest, rather than pull any shenanigans lower down. He starts his day counting pills prescribed for his numerous ailments, while wishing for a successful visit to the porcelain throne. His late-afternoon routine after a round of golf includes dabs of Old Spice in strategic areas, as he hopes for a surprise visit from one of the many casserole cooks. Yet this perfected prodigy is not going to settle for just anyone. He's as alert as feathered fowl in a Louisiana swamp, scurrying away at just the right moment to escape

a creeping crocodile's jaws. The crafty
looker says the only alligator he likes is a
Hermès Birkin stuffed with greenbacks.

~~~~~~~~~

<p align="center">This lover dreams only
of a personal Florence
Nightingale, the one woman
never to cause him any
stress.</p>

~~~~~~~~~

 He doesn't mind an expanded torso
or pendulous breasts. What is most
important to this aging Woody Allen is
that whomever rests beside him only
does so after spooning his laxative and
making it easy for him to swallow. Forget
Sophia Loren. This lover dreams only
of a personal Florence Nightingale,
the one woman never to cause him any
stress. She lives only to serve his ever-
growing neediness. It's true. He is the old
geezer playing gin rummy with his fellow
Saturday night assisted living refugees
and talking about landing a new honey.

He knows she would be better than the poorly paid attendants at this joint. "Look, you chumps," he says as he lays down a winning hand, "the best retirement is having a woman who takes care of you. Start looking now before you're strapped to a gurney, wishing you hadn't forgotten your cholesterol medicine all those nights you spend alone."

~~~~~~~~~

"The best retirement is having a woman who takes care of you."

~~~~~~~~~

Granted, this neurotic nerd isn't going to be found guilty of paying the cable company for the adult-only channels. Instead, he is more likely to flip through medical journals and nursing school registers for fun. He may even occasionally attend graduation ceremonies for nearby RN programs, hoping to entice an older returning college student to accompany him to Starbucks for a celebration coffee. A careful study of his

Facebook reveals he "friends" only those in the medical community.

~~~~~~~~~

He is the dandy devil dressed to the nines who is perfectly positioned at every charity fete.

~~~~~~~~~

You know this man has no interest in a lover for he cannot bear the thought of popping one more pill. Viagra is of no use for him, but a woman wearing a stethoscope arouses some far away stirring. Unlike his younger days when a woman in a nurse's uniform would sometimes tickle a fantasy, he now wishes to find a real life WW II retiree with an up-to-date licensed care certificate. Sex is for the young, he has concluded, but a nurse is always in demand.

Sirens, if your ex left you plenty of silver in the bank vault, or if your daddy's will willed you a two-week Italian Riviera cruise and money for your own Mercedes, be especially wise to this pie-eyed prowler. He is the dandy devil dressed to the nines who is perfectly positioned at every charity fete. Teeth whitening strips toppling out of his topcoat, he's often seen gurgling Listerine in the men's room during the Sotheby's auctions. He is the polished purveyor of only the finest. Dual fisted, he downs a flute of Dom Pérignon while dispatching the bill to his dinner date.

If you should be so unlucky as to meet him, expect to be schmoozed as he reaches for your Cartier-clad fingers in a sweeping gesture and an ensuing delicate smooch. He is skilled.

Dual fisted, he downs a flute of Dom Pérignon while dispatching the bill to his dinner date.

Often graduating first in class at the Arthur Murray Studio, he is not shy on the dance floor. Gliding you past the envious eyes of your boarding school classmates, his eyes are fixed on you. Like a Fortune 500 CEO, although with no known employment, this Don Juan is driven.

Never one to waste time on broke, buxom beauties, he takes great pride in having plenty of time to woo his prey without having to worry about work commitments. His full-time job is finding the next well-endowed dowager, and he considers a woman's best attribute to be a bulging bank account.

He takes great pride in having plenty of time to woo his prey without having to worry about work commitments.

Not surprisingly, he keeps his CD changer tuned to his favorite lullaby, Roy Orbison's "Only the Lonely." This savvy salesman knows the loneliest

lovers are the most likely to pay off his
overdrawn accounts at Bergdorf's and
keep him supplied in caviar and French
champagne. After all, hunting with his
intensity takes a lot of energy. His butler
can relieve some of the stress until he
bags another big bankroll. By then, his
current situation may be somewhat sullied.
Another coffer may need to be attended!

Walkers Aren't for Rehab

B abbling during bridge is
commonplace among divas
discussing upcoming dinner dances
and delving into details they shouldn't.

"God," says one of the girls, "I'm glad
I'm married, but I have to say it's getting
old having Tom trouncing my twinkle toes
during the two-step. Tripping me during
my twirl is his best move." The ladies sigh
a knowing sigh, sadly recalling the dismal
dance moves of their own mates as you,
the Single Siren, come into view at the
country club.

You silently swallow, knowing their
pontification is about to pounce. Eyes slid
southward to avert their stares, you endure
an awkward moment before the boldest
one belts out, "So who is taking *you* to the
soirée?" You stammer before awkwardly
admitting that you don't yet have a date
for the dance. Instantly, shame and
humiliation become your soul sisters while
the card-playing coterie tries consoling
you with unusually sincere condolences.

"You're a savvy single," suggests one.
"What you need is a walker."

You wince. "A walker?" you think. "I don't think so. I've always had excellent posture."

"You're a savvy single," suggests one. "What you need is a walker."

"Silly girl," they gush. To your astonishment, you learn they are not suggesting a rehab contraption but merely a man to lend you his arm while entering the affair. "He's an acceptable soul who can serve as your date without strings, darling," one summarizes. "His only demand is a free ticket and a sufficient supper."

A walker sounds wonderful, but what's a Siren to do to secure this sexy chaperone? "Does anyone know someone who fits this bill?" you instantly inquire. You're open to opportunities. First, Mary Jane suggests her sister-in-law's brother. The only problem, she notes, could be his crazy ex who's known for conspicuously crashing any celebration.

Gladys gladly offers her favorite cousin who suffers from intermittent constipation. Depending on him for a definite date might be a disaster, you think. Although you're decidedly depressed deciphering these disappointing details, you soldier on.

Although you're decidedly depressed deciphering these disappointing details, you soldier on.

"Anyone else have an offering?" You remain hopeful.

"I know a gorgeous guy who would be great," gushes Georgia Sue. The divas seem relieved with her revelation and immediately look to you for affirmation. They are obviously interested in your assessment, so you want to play this one right.

"Yes…" you guardedly profess. "He might be the perfect partner." You force a fake smile and inquire more about his assets. Walks upright? Check! Absence of Alzheimer's? Check! Can commandeer a car? Check! This man, you ruminate, might be right for you, but it's not until your grandfather's guidance erupts in your ears that you know are game. "Nothing ventured, nothing gained," he always said. "Go for it, goddess!" echoes your gut. Straight or gay, men can be genteel and generous companions, and you determine that you need a walker regardless of his sexual persuasion.

"Is it the Donald descending my steps?" You're not sure if it's a helmet or his abhorrent hairline.

When the big night finally arrives, the mantel clock's tick tock reminds you that your new Prince Charming should be wheeling his chariot in your driveway

momentarily. Georgia Sue has assured
you that he is heterosexual and ready to
cohabit. You tense a bit thinking of the last
loser you were lucky to lose after whisking
him away from the kittens at the bar. That
experience was short lived, but your love
lost was heaven sent, as it turns out. Don't
sigh, Siren, you have a sixth sense with
sexual suitors. Remember, you're in the
driver's seat now.

Remember, you're in the
driver's seat now.

The car door slams. You stare between
the window shades. "Oh dear God," you
think upon first glance. "Is it the Donald
descending my steps?" You're not sure if
it's a helmet or his abhorrent hairline. Your
memory sharpens as you recall attending
an earlier event with another escort. You'd
considered his odd coiffure was due to
a bevy of belligerent cowlicks. However
upon entering the event, a cooling fan's
short blast had ruffled his rug and his
tousled toupee landed in the lap of the

local newspaper's social scribe! The two
of you tripped across the gala's threshold
while he desperately tried to trap his tuft.
The wind won and your peacock's plume
was forever plucked. Blowing in the wind
was now not a once-popular song, but
your man's head merkin sailing across the
red carpet!

Often, divas will do swan dives to be
subsumed in the social section of the daily.
Not you! After that dandy Don defrocked
himself in front of the unforgiving camera
lens, your photo on his arm was plastered
across the newspaper's pages. Now you
slink away from the shutterbugs. And your
"got your back" girlfriends still gleefully
goad you over this social gaffe.

It's no wonder then that fear strikes
your heart as this newest eager entrant is
struggling to tidy his tousled tendrils as he
teeters toward your door. You reluctantly
recall your memories of hair hell. Whether
Trump tresses or turbulent toupees, your
will for a "walker" has suddenly waned.

On impulse, you adopt the demeanor
of an infectious invalid. You fake a

hacking cough as the doorbell harkens.
Standing near the entrance you heighten
your hawking. Surely this buffoon can
hear your barking! Through the door,
you ask him to depart quickly as you've
likely been invaded by Ebola. He
startles, stammers, and hurriedly steps
away. "I'm...so...sorry," he stutters.

The moral to this story, Siren, is this:
there's no need for a walker while you can
still stand steadily and open your own
doors!

Sex is Confusing

If you found your way to single status by way of divorce, you may find this scene familiar. It's 1:00 A.M. and you're suffering through rearranged sleeping patterns after the divorce. For the first time since you separated, you begin perusing dating sites, and the computer screen welcomes your intrusion. Your heart flutters with excitement, and the many possibilities an Internet love site offers boggle your mind. Yada, yada, yada, what's a girl to do?

For the first time since you separated, you begin perusing dating sites.

A little birdie chirps in your head, "Sign up, stupid. Your psyche needs a massage." You commit to a website, and it begins to do some snooping of its own. You dutifully answer the electronic busybody's details, as its continuous questions get more curious.

Who are you attracted to?
"That should be easy," you think.
"Probably someone like my previous
scoundrel." After all, you've always been
a creature of habit.

~~~~~~~~

You tell yourself being a
cougar is okay and that your
kids will be fine with it.

~~~~~~~~

You feel safe checking the white male
heterosexual box. Next this prying portal
dares to ask something else. *How old are
you?* "Hmmm," you think, " let's push the
envelope here." You tell yourself being
a cougar is okay and that your kids will
be fine with it. You briefly consider that
40–70 years is a big range, but you're a
cool chick and it's nobody's business!

The potential choices seem
innumerable. *Will you be willing
to engage in a relationship with a
Caucasian, one of European decent,
an African American, an Asian…?*

"Dear God," you think. "I guess we'll descend to eye color and number of body moles next." You continue to read the questionnaire and pray. You need to get this right, but the anxiety level is causing neck tension. How can a Siren emote eroticism to an iPhone 6 anyway?

You decide to be true to yourself and think deeply. Divorce does that.

Are you heterosexual, homosexual, bisexual, transgender...? My God, where did all these labels originate? Did Freud make up this stuff just to keep us confused? Or was it Jane Goodall after having a heat stroke observing copulating primates? "Whatever," you say. You decide to be true to yourself and think deeply. Divorce does that.

Next box. *What are your desired activities?* You suddenly feel as if it's your first time at a Baptist summer camp.

Swimming, sports, reading, needlepoint—
the example hobbies are endless. Finally
admitting to a rather simpleton self, you
realize that just want safe sex without
the male species snickering when you
undress. Yes, you need serious sex. And
much to your surprise, you are settling
for an electronic sex therapist in order to
achieve your aim.

You realize that just want
safe sex without the male
species snickering when you
undress.

"Now we're back to LGBT categories,"
you realize, silently celebrating personal
growth in the awareness of others' sexual
preferences. Various boxes waiting to be
checked affirm your flexibility as your
mind wanders to the Caesar's Palace pool
attendant you ogled during your divorce
party in Vegas. Regardless of his Internet
classification, your unfettered fantasies
went wild that weekend.

"Stop it!" you chastise yourself. "You must focus." Yet your mind continues to silently lecture your obvious absence of activities and scolds you for skulking around in the World Wide Web. But you're ensnared by the possibility of social scenarios now. You cannot shut down the sinister longings of a sexy Siren like yourself. You take a brief vow of silence on the subject of social media and determine to keep your single sisters unaware of your strategy.

You cannot shut down the sinister longings of a sexy Siren like yourself.

Send a profile picture, your personal PC stipulates. *Include your birth date*, the damnable desktop demands. This naughty network is taking over your life. Determined to skillfully manipulate the menacing device, you begin the search for a phenomenal photo. You know, the one that's fitting for your future.

Never a photogenic finalist at your prom, avoiding cameras has been your modus operandi, but now the nefarious screen before you is insisting on a shot. Not to be outsmarted, you recall your glory days getting your portrait at the mall. Perhaps the 1980s will pique the imagination of an electronic inamorato— an interested Internet intruder who could steal your heart and seal your fate.

Although it's with some trepidation, you decide you will not be deterred.

You revel in your reverie over a 20-year-old picture certain to dazzle any Don Juan. Delighted with your deviousness, a small concern arises that there could be danger lurking. A sex kitten like the one looking back at you in the photograph might lure too many losers. Although it's with some trepidation, you decide you will not be deterred. The birthdate question mark is easily quelled. Minus 20 years is simple to calculate. With a keystroke you shave off the ravages of two long decades of distress and hair dye.

Those who friend Facebook may feel superior, but online dating is something else altogether.

You secretly try not to worry that your gal pals might stumble upon your profile. "Surely not those spinsters," you assure yourself. Simple bridge games baffle them. Thus, being bound to a computer is unlikely. Those who friend Facebook may feel savvy, but online dating is something else altogether.

Okay, Ms. Socially Superior, it's time to push the button. Seize the day! Carpe diem! The future is yours! You reach for the digital digits as you enter your credit card number for the website membership fee. Your heart skips. Scared of being termed a super predator taking unfair advantage of weakened prey, you pause before pushing "continue."

Deceit is the work of the devil. Admit your age and revel in your wrinkles.

Something brushes your shoulder. It's now very late, and impossible to discern the garb, but you clearly see a man on your shoulder. Perhaps a priest, a preacher, or a padre—he stands ready to give you patriarchal pointers.

"Don't do it!" he dares to direct you. "Deceit is the work of the devil. Admit your age and revel in your wrinkles."

You have to concede that the pontiff is right. It's indecent to be deceitful. Feeling suddenly strong and superior, you add back the years in a flash. Without brutal honesty, a Siren's honor will hit the road.

You instantly feel relief. Never one to double cross or double deal, you deal the hand you've been given. If the desktop Dandy Dons dabble on the keys looking only for youthful divas, you won't bat an eye.

~~~~~~~~~

Breaking free from the threat of Internet addiction, you show superior strength.

~~~~~~~~~

Breaking free from the threat of Internet addiction, you show superior strength. Snap, snap, you turn off the tantalizing terminal. Tonight, you admit to having pride in your principles. Impeccable integrity is your mate, but who knows what's next in the wild world of Internet dating? Carnal desires could make you cave. After all, as Miss Scarlett declared, "Tomorrow is another day."

Wired in a Web of Lies

If you are somewhat provincial, believing that if you are true to your man he should hold the same standard, you might want to pay attention to his cell phone and computer habits. If your lover carries his phone to the bathroom and you hear nothing but the pitter-patter of quick clicks, odds are high that he's a double dealing duplicitous dude dialing up a secretive soon-to-be sweetie.

When the two of you are entwined on your sleeper sofa watching *America's Most Wanted* and you notice his mobile device is lighting up decrying a possible deception, you have three choices. If you want to keep him in your clutches long enough to see John Walsh capture another hoodlum, simply ignore it and hope he is oblivious to her texts.

Another option is to say, "You have a message," with your sweet voice cooing like chocolate syrup dripping on his collar. Then watch his demeanor with the intuition of a James Bond femme fatale. If he gets anxious and loosens his grip around any of your body parts he had been interested in prior to your purr, you'll know this cat just received an invitation to go on the prowl. He may even excuse himself to your powder room so he can text the temptress and make a hasty retreat under the pretense of stomach pains.

The third scenario is to confront your procurer of pretense. In this case, Siren, hold your ground. When you boldly ask whether he is texting another woman, expect a myriad of responses.

> When you boldly ask whether he is texting another woman, expect a myriad of responses.

You have decisions to make. Regardless of which option you choose, knowing how to handle this male handful can be harrowing. What should you do when the next radiating ringtone ruminates in your psyche? Let's play out a scenario where your man appears to be wired in a web of lies and see how it goes.

Always one of grace, let's say you believe in second chances. You decide that scheduling dinner again with the Google geek will guide your technological tactics. Throughout the meal, you remain acutely attuned to any ring, reverberation, or racket coming from his pocket. All is quiet, so why is he suddenly sliding out his chair and announcing a bathroom break?

~~~~~~~

Always one of grace, let's say you believe in second chances.

~~~~~~~

"Did he get receive a toot from his tata and you were tuned out?" you wonder, questioning your hearing acumen. It certainly seems that you must have somehow missed her signal for him to scramble for his device and dash for distance. Fifteen minutes fly by and your fraudulent fellow returns flustered.

Clearly irritated, you directly inquire, "Did you get a sudden message that demanded your attention?" Stammering, he stumbles over his syllables. "No," the nervous nerd nods.

Your fervent inclination to absolve his absence forces you to forgive his table manners. Maybe you've been too suspicious when he slips away to the men's room. Your prince may have a prostate problem demanding his sudden departures. This possibility does deserve your consideration, as there were no perceptible blares, blasts, or blows from his communication beast.

A little flirting might cool his need for all other conquests.

After dessert, you determine to amp up your allure. A little flirting might cool his need for all other conquests. You inch nearer to his body, lightly laying your hand on his leg and leaving your trust issues on your therapist's couch. You scoot even closer, thighs touching, pat his arm and slide your hand in his pocket. Your

pulse is beating harder now, electricity in
the air.

That's when his leg begins vibrating
violently, a veritable lightshow emanating
from his pants. You bolt backward, shocked
by the sheer power of your Siren sexuality.
This man is putty in your hands now.

But suddenly he stands erect.
Shimmying out of the booth, he bolts for
the bathroom again. This time you realize
what's happened. This cad's cell phone
is on vibrate mode and the flirty female
has been flashing in his pocket all night.
"That's it!" you tell yourself. Sirens like
you don't need sleazy suitors. You've had
enough for one evening and decide to
make your own dash for the door.

Golden Acres

Harry was left with little after his divorce. Without the homemaking necessities you brought to the marriage, he would have been stuck with instant coffee and protein bars. As older lovers, Sirens might have some cellulite and gray hairs, but they are also more likely to own their own Nespresso machine and a Cuisinart. You bailed him out of bachelorhood, and all you expected from your plucked rooster was access to his intact 401k and a share of his well-earned Social Security check. The ex-witch had secured weekly manicured digits on these entitlements, and a new wife should be entitled also.

Your two and a half years as Harry's last wife were blissful. The family blended nicely, and all was ideal until your later-in-life-lover keeled over one day while spearing a slice of brisket at the country club's Friday night all-you-can-eat buffet. What a shocker! Being single again was not in your plans. But here you are, misty eyed while reviewing your angel's burial plan with the smiling vice president of the Golden Acres Cemetery Association.

"Mrs. Smith," he utters, his pearly whites beaming directly into your cataracts, "your husband left his afterlife wishes in writing. I have a copy right here."

~~~~~~

As older lovers, Sirens might have some cellulite and gray hairs, but they are also more likely to own their own Nespresso machine and a Cuisinart.

~~~~~~

"Good," you think, "this should be easy. I just want to be sure our gravesites are adjacent. I'll keep his and mine weeded and always with a fresh bouquet!"

"Mrs. Smith," interrupts the interpreter of last rites, "I need to share something with you."

Startled by his authoritative tone infringing upon your grief, you suddenly realize that this death business is serious.

"This man is telling me what my Harry wants," you think, certain you already know what Harry wanted. "I'll humor him, but what I really need to be doing is making my pedicure appointment." You need to look good at the funeral. After all, his ex-wife and some of her family might show up.

Your plans were to spend more time cruising and spending his kids' inheritance.

"Your husband," the obvious shareholder in Brylcreem begins again, "never changed his desires to be buried by Mrs. Smith."

"Well, of course he didn't," you conclude. You and Harry broached the death issue a few times but never belabored the details. Your plans were to spend more time cruising and spending his kids' inheritance.

"Mrs. Smith," Mr. Golden Acres persists once more in derailing your train of thought, "I am talking about the last Mrs. Smith." He gulps. "I think her name is Betty..." Another gulp and a glance at his notes. "Yes, her name is Betty."

"Whaaaaat?" you shriek.

The "louse" that woman so vehemently described to the divorce judge while securing all loose assets for her new nest somehow also secured her afterlife! She got the burial plot they purchased while still in wedded bliss. It wasn't enough for her to take your poor Harry for far too much alimony. She kept the lovely house and the good silver too! What she didn't keep, his greedy children picked over like newborn chickens grubbing for kernels of corn.

So Harry wants to be buried by Betty? What about you? Are you to be covered with daisies on the west parking lot while their fancy marble headstones frolic together in afterlife lust? The ex will rest in Golden Acres' lap of luxury while you, the beleaguered last wife, are left with only

94

an aging coffee pot and memories? This cannot be!

Mr. Golden Acres explains that the plans state that you are to be buried on top of Betty. Disappointed is not the word for your mental state. Severely pissed off is more like it! Mr. Golden Acres busies himself shuffling through his papers, allowing you time for a tantrum. Devastated by the thought of Harry being back with her for eternity, you choke back tears. Once again, the last wife is last again. What's a Siren to do?

You hurriedly consider your options.

I can hardly demand that Harry allow me to lie on top of him for perpetuity. After all, we both shared claustrophobia.
Maybe I could squeeze in beside him. Either side will suffice. That way I could once again come between him and her!

Mr. Golden Acres wants to move on to discussing the funeral arrangements, but how can you lead the funeral processional like a seasoned pro while knowing the former Mrs. Harry has not an once of genuine concern behind her little hankie and tear-strewn makeup? His precious ones will be delighted that their perfect dad will once again be with their perfect mom. Yeah, that darned woman wins again.

Never one to be buried alive by bad news, you dab your mascara and stiffen your neck. You will not be beaten. If this is the way it is, at least you went out on top! Long live the Siren!

The Check is
in the Mail

Well, how wrong were you? Never having dealt with death, only divorce, Harry's departure has been devastating. An appointment with the funeral director and his bookkeeper seemed simple enough. Wrong again!

When you'd gone yesterday to the funeral home to make arrangements, the undertaker had inquired, "Mrs. Smith, how do you plan to pay for Mr. Smith's interment?"

"Wow," you'd thought, "this guy has a surprising command of big words!"

You were very businesslike in your response, saying, "Harry and I had some savings, and also I will receive his Social Security check. I can sign next month's payment over to you."

"How long were you married?" Mr. Inquisitive had pried.

"Two and a half blissful years," you'd bragged, feeling self-satisfied in comparison to today's fly by night unions.

Mr. Inquisitive was nonplussed. "Mrs. Smith, you need to call the Social Security office and establish your benefits since your husband has passed." The Golden Acres gatekeeper then added, "Also, please check with your bank to determine how your account is held." Slightly irritated with his demands (and the implication that your bank account might not be what you thought), you'd agreed to calculate the worth of your singledom and left his office with your mind reeling.

~~~~~~

As you wheel into the gray government edifice, you are composed. Being protected by the US government is a special feeling.

~~~~~~

Now with the funeral just a few days away, you have little time to maneuver. First stop, the Social Security office. As you wheel into the gray government edifice, you are composed. Being protected by the US government is a special feeling. After all, Harry was productive and likely qualified for the maximum government stipend. "This should be a piece of cake," you assure yourself.

While reaching for a number to be attended to, a woman your age peels off her wedding ring and throws it at the clerk. "Goodness," you murmur softly and internally scold the scoundrel behind the counter. This is no place for lover's spats. Little do you know that what you've just witnessed is a very bad omen.

Little do you know that what you've just witnessed is a very bad omen.

Two hours and twenty-five minutes later, the loudspeaker bellows, "Mrs. Smith, desk four." Having slipped into a sleepy state while sitting upright, you startle.

"Yes, that's me," you offer in a friendly voice, settling into a chair in front of desk four.

"What can I do for you?" Miss Efficiency wants to know.

Confused, you smile, thinking how the entire world has suddenly become engrossed with your betrothal.

"My beloved Harry died, and I need to transfer his monthly check to my name." Simple enough, you assess. Wrong again!

After prolonged computer key clicking, she asks the same question the funeral director asked. "How long were you married?"

Confused, you smile, thinking how the entire world has suddenly become engrossed with your betrothal. "Two and a half blissful years," you declare. Her silence is deafening. Her brow furrows and her fingers stroke the digits ever more forcefully. Your breathing becomes shallow.

"I'm sorry, Mrs. Smith. You won't qualify for his checks. Your marriage was too short!"

"What? What do you mean I don't qualify?"

"You don't qualify. Mr. Smith's first wife will receive his benefits for the rest of her life. That is, unless she remarries."

You are supposed to be the surviving spouse. You're the one who nursed Harry during his dying days.

"Fat chance of that happening," you think. "That dame will milk this situation the rest of her days. Any loving she does will be sans a wedding ring." How could this be? You are supposed to be the surviving spouse. You're the one who nursed Harry during his dying days. Your friends reported seeing "her" lunching at Neiman Marcus while you ate off Harry's tray. Her bridge game became legendary, while your gray hair outgrew its tint as you remained by Harry's side. She's been seen with a much younger tomcat, while your beloved could barely whisper, "I love you."

Miss Efficiency has shown you to the door by now, and you find yourself feeling lightheaded as you make your way across the parking lot to your car. "Life is not fair," you lament as you start your vehicle. But who can you confide in about your troubles without looking selfish and pitiful? You know. You'll talk to God. Closing your eyes tightly and gripping the steering wheel, you begin to pray.

God, first, please bless Harry and make sure he looks down on me as the one who made him comfortable. Bless me and take this bitterness away in the next hour while I get my roots retouched. And God, I know I'm not supposed to ask for bad things to happen, but if "she" comes to see Harry

at the visitation, could you make sure her
cellulite is showing? I just want Harry to
see her for who she is. Is that too much to
ask? Amen.

To Sex or Not to Sex

The social mores of the new millennium have skewed and confused the ancient advice passed down by generations of mothers to their daughters. You were the lucky recipient of age-old wisdom concerning carnal knowledge. It was a lazy, hot summer day sitting with your overprotective mother on your family's front porch. While she dutifully mended the elbows of your brother's cotton shirts, she had asserted, "If you want to catch a man, don't have sex until your wedding night."

You were startled. The pseudo-saintly seamstress had entered virgin ground. Discussions of any sexual content were routinely closeted within your Ozzie and Harriet upbringing. Shocked by your mother's infinite grasp of all things physical, your cheeks went afire thinking of your boyfriend's unzipped jeans. You meekly nodded. Discussion over!

Thirty-five years of marriage and three lovely children (other than when they are acting like their father) later, you are facing another copulation crisis. Your mother's savvy "snare the sucker with delayed sex" is ringing like tinnitus in your ears. Obviously you and your virginal halo were dethroned the first night with Fred oh so many years ago. But you simply weren't prepared for your newest paramour to bring up "making love next weekend." "How delicate," you'd thought at his suggestion. Making love sounds like some love-struck teen willing to ignore the hairy armpits of her suitor while scrambling in the dark. What your lover really means is, "Let's have sex."

~~~~~~~~

Your mother's savvy "snare the sucker with delayed sex" is ringing like tinnitus in your ears.

~~~~~~~~

Several sexless nights have elapsed since encountering your new Don Juan at Sunday school. You had prayed diligently, asking God to give you love. Now, with Don Juan's plans for next weekend, you mentally note to find out if God's confused also. You asked for love, and instead he is offering you an oversexed Cialis-soaked senior.

Now's the time, Siren! To sex or not to sex, this is the question.

Though it's true that a sexy Siren simply can't keep the men from flocking to her, this one wants to roost in your nest. He wants to be the "cock of the walk" and being a product of his post-divorce counseling sessions, he isn't ashamed to ask you to deliver on his desires.

This newest dilemma demands that you ditch your diet pills and down a few donuts in order to up your dopamine level.

Heretofore, your own trusted therapist had advised you to reside in a single woman's stress free environment. This newest dilemma demands that you ditch your diet pills and down a few donuts in order to up your dopamine level. "I've got decisions to make," you declare, justifying your splurge.

~~~~~~~~~

It is obvious your newest interest never invested in Rogaine or a hair transplant.

~~~~~~~~~

You knew the sex thing would ensue. Not a spinster, you realize a man's body could relight your libido, but this weekend's offering has some obvious objections. The Sunday school sexual advertisement offering you instant love has limitations to consider. Never one to seek a roll in the hay with the rotund, you're reeling from the visual. Fred was not Arnold Schwarzenegger, but he did maintain a pittance of firm pecs. Plus, he had a full head of hair. It is obvious your newest interest never invested in Rogaine or a hair transplant. His pelo went packing, skipping his skull and landing

on his legs, rendering him genetically
related to Bigfoot.

<hr />

You want your soul sisters to swoon when they see your seductive seducer.

<hr />

Distressed by his defects, you
decide this one is a no. Yes, make that
a "no way"! Yet you determine to keep
searching, conceding privately that you
suffer from a newfound egotism. You
admit that your new man must possess
phenomenal (or at least passable)
physical traits. It's imperative that he
present well at the Saturday evening
supper club. You want your soul sisters
to swoon when they see your seductive
seducer. But how to tell him the bad news?

Accepting his Saturday lunch date
offer, you're fully aware that today is
D-Day. You'll deliver the death knell
during dessert. But why is Mr. Would Be
wooing you so wonderfully, you wonder?

Mentally preparing to wound his desires, you start to detest yourself. After all, he is *such* a nice guy. Sipping your cappuccino, you find you cannot avert your gaze from his great smile. His hands appear nimble and capable of arousing even your spinster aunt. He is obviously interested in your every word, signaling a sincerity Fred never shared. You also have to admit that his dancing skills are such that every diva desires.

Maybe it's true...baldies are better in bed.

You feel your resolve retiring. Maybe it's true...baldies are better in bed. A little layer of adipose might adequately warm your soul and other stirrings. Why not dive into the dating sexual scene with an affable chap who doesn't demand perfection when a simple yes will do?

Who needs all those Adonis types displaying their toned, tanned torsos? What you need is chicken soup and apple pie. Besides, you can forget your own foibles while romping in the sack with him. Unfettered fat cells can maintain residence on your thighs. Wrinkles residing on your forehead are fine. Going lower on the perfection cycle is freeing! You can be yourself and wrap your furry robe around your cellulite afterward. He will likely be lounging and trying to regain his lung capacity anyway.

"Okay," you think. "I am going to upend my upbringing, defy Mother's advice, and go for the gold! Let's go all the way!"

Your decision made, lingering memories of the stud in high school English class unexpectedly rush through your body. Studying Shakespeare was a joy in the presence of that high school heartthrob. It was "To Sex or Not to Sex?" when you were fifteen. How some things never change. Your Siren status affords you the same Shakespearean question after every date. To Sex or Not to Sex? That is still the question.

Sex Takes Stamina

Gosh darn. It's yoga class again today. Three times a week is about all you can muster. Ever the optimist, you're certain your downward dog stance may be vital in case your latest lover gets creative. You're prepared for most anything these days.

Having lots of time on your hands since your last troubled tryst, you've embarked on a complete course of tantric enhancing education. You pity those poor bridge buddies of yours. They spend far too much time eating lemon squares and making surly demands that their female partners play more defensively. You've always been a smart cookie. You've been dedicated to educating your mind and developing your body for singlehood. After reading tidbits designed to attract a true love, you decide you'll proudly wear the title "temptress" if it means mortal men will be mush under the spell of your carnal knowledge.

Your mama always said the way to a man's heart is through his stomach. But being a naive princess who married too young, little did you know his stomach has a direct effect on his private parts.

For example, one of the first things you discover is the proud pronouncement of pumpkin seeds as penis enhancers. "What? That's easy," you think. Any future dinner at your place will serve little clumps of the stuff hidden in a menu designed for maximum sexual function. Then your yoga poses will pay off handsomely.

Cherry pie and a glass of red wine should put him in the mood for moving the sheets.

The second commonly known libido lifter you discover is the goddess of the sea: oysters. These little puppies pack a punch in the man's pouch. Your partner's sex drive will soar after a six-pack of these shellfish, according to the magazines. Red cherries— yummy!—can also aid your ability to improve your sex life through his stomach. Cherry pie and a glass of red wine should put him in the mood for moving the sheets. Armed with these physical accouterments and schooled in the art of seduction, your next lady-killer will be easy prey for your enlightened libido.

Two requisite sexless dates behind you, you've invited the beguiled but ignorant inamorato for a third date for dinner at your place. He smells sex in the air. Yoga has whittled an inch or two, allowing you to wear your low cut wrap dress. (It's so easy to unwrap!) The scent of cherry pie wafts through the kitchen, pumpkin seeds innocently hide under the ranch dressing, and chilled oysters beg to be between his recently flossed pearly whites.

You sweep down the short steps, *Donna Reed Show* style.

The doorbell signals a surrender. He's arrived. You sweep down the short steps, *Donna Reed Show* style. You plant a kiss on the cheek, not too sexy, but a promise of more after his tummy is warm and satisfied.

You seat yourself to his right, never letting your adoring gaze leave his gluttonous gorging. The scarfing of your sex samples surprises you as he stuffs his face with your sustenance. Your goal was not to assure his livelihood but merely to enhance his libido.

You gulp but never divert your attention. "Ingesting all of the exciting edibles has surely excited his eroticism and his manhood must be on the rise by now," you think as you practice your yoga breathing techniques. You will not waste all this carefully planned perfection.

That's when he sits back and belches, not a burp, but a bellow. You bolt from the chair, immediately proposing a move to the couch. He shuffles your way, unhinging his torso from the table with discomfort. "The cherries must be gurgling," you surmise. He smiles and moves laboriously toward you.

Think fast, Siren. You've worked hard for this moment. Is your fitness level worth the cost of lessons at Yoga Hut? The next hour could determine your financial

commitment's efficacy. You suggest coyly
that he move to the bedroom and take
off his shoes. No man can resist this ploy.
He plops and you pull off each alligator
leather shoe, realizing quickly those
reptiles are a sweaty mess. Wrap dresses
are known for gaping open and yours is
no stranger to this mishap. He is not dead.
He grins.

"There's always another
day," you console yourself.
"And more than one yoga
class in this town."

A little foreplay later, you lightly hop
on top. "I've got the yoga moves," you
think and smile to yourself. He grunts, but
no appendage is available for any kind
of usage. Maybe a downward dog will
deliver the vinegar to revive his virility?
You grind, much like the "reptile pose"
you've mastered in class. He just sighs
and begins to apologize. You persist a
minute more, thinking of how many zeros

the cash register chimed at the Whole Foods in preparation for this futile exercise session. But he shimmies to shake you off his lackluster loins. You dismount. Ride over. Game over!

He rolls off your 800-count Egyptian cotton sheets and slips back into his sweaty slippers. He again attempts an apology and you, always with class, touch his shoulder and declare no foul. "Let's get together again," you say in the hallway. Sirens have been known to stretch the truth to save another's feelings.

He scurries out the door, and you rattle the dishes and scrape your plates. He licked his clean as a whistle. "There's always another day," you console yourself. "And more than one yoga class in this town." You determine to go to the one that has men in the class. Then you start scheming. "I'm going to put my yoga mat so close to the unsuspecting oaf that I can touch his hand during the stretching and offer him some pumpkin seeds afterwards for forgiveness!"

Can These Kids Be His?

Pussy-whipped. This is the term used many times for a man who is utterly and hopelessly controlled by his wife. But is there a word for a parent who is utterly and hopelessly controlled by his adult children?

After a few romantic dates with your sexy sweetheart, you both agreed it was time to meet the families. It was not the time for earth-shattering announcements but simply a lead-in to later possibilities since it has been going swimmingly well with your suitor.

~~~~~~

But is there a word for a parent who is utterly and hopelessly controlled by his adult children?

~~~~~~

Although your Don Juan dons them "the little darlins," decades have passed since their earthly entrance. His descendants decided on the date, time, and dinner place, leaving you feeling as though a late in life lobotomy had limited your capabilities. "Keep the peace at all costs," counseled your costly counselor. So you tried.

There's just one problem. Their eatery of choice specializes in Thai. For you, this signals impending disaster. Your last Thai adventure aggravated your allergies and offered you an overnighter with a shot of epinephrine in the regional care facility. Orderlies had scribbled DOA on your sheets. Helpless to overturn your prognosis, you're still thanking the overweight LVN who finally captured your pulse.

After all, newbies and third wheels are merely rough-edged appendages in well-oiled family circles.

You cannot attend Thai. You gingerly offered an alternative to your lover, thinking he would humor you. But he gasped for air, able to utter but a few syllables. "Oh no," he scolded. Catching his breath, he continued, "The kids love Thai. I always go wherever they choose. I've trained them to make great choices." You realize that unless you choose to invoke the rules of war and instigate another Pearl Harbor, you'd better go along to get along. After all, newbies and third wheels are merely rough-edged appendages in well-oiled family circles.

Sneaking two diet fudge bars into your oversized bag, you gaily enter the den of poison on the said date. Your allergic reaction merely quivers in anticipation of another overnight date with a handsome orderly stretched out on a gurney.

Approaching the table containing the cosseted kids, you conceal your dinner bars and extend your palm. Being a savvy one, you instantly discern sabotage and torpedoes lurking beneath their designer jeans. Two pampered princesses and an overly spoiled male oaf slide out of their seats. Half-slit smiles and slight head nods can't hide their intent to harm.

"Hi," you manage to chirp, hoping they will see your enthusiasm and just maybe realize you aren't the sister of New York convict, Leona Helmsley. Even with years of corporate experience reading your business associates, this crew appears to have trained with the KGB. Do they hate you or just have severe headaches? Their defense is impossible to penetrate.

Ever one to persevere in the face of danger, you still plan to deliver a delightful dinner demeanor. Although Asian cuisine is your archenemy, you will remain calm in the presence of enemy combatants. Sirens, you remember, have experience on their side. Daddy's ducklings cannot turn this into a disaster. Decorum is your forte. Your smile would impress Picasso, your perspective is perky, and your social skills superb.

Meanwhile, smoke billows from the backroom Thai kitchen as diminutive waiters deliver steaming servings, but your table is ensconced in ice. At the risk of riling the ASPCA, you will remember to consider a fur coat if there is another encounter with this condescending clan.

130

Proud papa bear beams, looking over his brood. "Aren't they perfect?" he purrs in your ear.

~~~~~~

Always honest with yourself, you admit, "They want me gone."

~~~~~~

You smile feebly and feign agreement. Always honest with yourself, you admit, "They want me gone." Feeling particularly isolated in the polar ice cap, you start to become defensive. "I'm a nice person, aren't I? Why would these pampered progenies want to prevent my pleasure? What have I done to provoke such unpleasantness?"

Once more your therapist's words wind through your brain waves. *Don't let others manipulate you. Keep your core intact.* Sirens, beware. These poor pitiful souls are not your party. Read the situation's shorthand and dislodge your soul from this gaggle of ghastly ghouls—and quickly.

Suddenly you no longer see your committed comrade as your soul mate, but instead you see him as he really is. He's scared of his shadow and more scared of his relatives' wrath. This sad sack's shallowness will perpetually prevent him from finding happiness with anyone not blood bonded. He will forever be manipulated and mauled by his coddled coterie and yet always make excuses for their rude and offensive behavior. Why? Because he cannot accept that his bloodline might be blemished. He will not allow their abhorrent acts to sully his sick soul. Therefore, he must excuse their nasty nuances, fooling himself first and thinking he's fooling others.

You've been salvaged, Siren. They showed you their repugnant repertoire before you'd invested too much in these nauseating nascents. You are free and can now resume your search for a real man and real father who can honestly assess himself and his offspring. Sometimes a glass slipper cuts your toe, and this one is too painful.

Bulging Baggage

The three of you are having dinner: you, your new man, and Baggage. Your heavy load of past dating experiences over the past few months possibly weighs more than your new paramour. Mr. New Relationship cracks a clever remark, both bright and well timed. You chuckle, but Baggage smirks. "Don't let this latter day Don Juan deceive you. You can bet he's definitely screwed up," whispers your ever-present alarmist.

~~~~~~

The three of you are having dinner: you, your new man, and Baggage.

~~~~~~

Although you were happily enjoying your Beef Wellington just moments before, suddenly clouds crowd your psyche. You eyeball this imposter as though he's carrying the Zika virus. The turned-up corners of his mouth and his perfected smile should please your senses. Instead, they now make your hair raise, spine chill, and blood curdle.

Mr. Baggage is pleased with his progress, and the cautious comrade continues mentally lecturing you on not letting down your guard. "That's right," forewarns your familiar alter ego, "this guy is smooth and experienced. He's likely to leave you when you least expect it. Just when you've turned on your love lights—wham—he'll flip the lights off."

Still, you must admit that the gorgeous man sitting next to you is quite a catch. Looks, money, and a fun personality. You take another bite and smile across the table at your date, ignoring Baggage.

"No one is that perfect. Something's got to be wrong!" your sinister shadow shouts all the louder, crossing his arms and sitting satisfied in his chair.

Your resolve slowly starts to crack. "Well, maybe I am getting in too deep with this dastardly darling," you think. You decide to proceed carefully through dessert. You lightly chuckle at his chatter and try not to touch knees under the table, fully realizing your Medicare only pays 80 percent if infected by a strange disease.

But this guy's charm is contagious, and he draws you in with his attention. That's when Baggage furiously starts kicking at your ankles.

No more fear of flying and no room for a carry-on.

A ménage à trois has never interested you, so someone has to go. Repeated sessions with your trusted therapist have finally convinced you to bid adieu to your wounded wingman. "Time for this old girl to soar," you tell yourself as your man gets the check and you head out for the rest of your evening. "No more fear of flying and no room for a carry-on." Baffled by this turn of events, Baggage sulkily stays behind.

Now it's Saturday night and a new, lightweight you awaits. You're ready for love. No preconceived judgement, you feel energized, excited, and exhilarated about the evening ahead with your man. You put on your new Victoria's Secret underthings.

This could be the night.

A light knock at your door a few minutes early means your new man must be anxious to see you. You peek out the drapes but see no one on the stoop. Before you can blink, that old feeling of self-doubt seeps under the doorway like poisonous gas. It's Baggage again! You shudder to think the vacationer has returned...and he has brought friends with him. Fear, apprehension, and lack of confidence are tagging along.

Your new lover is lugging his own luggage—and it's a heavy load.

"Nope, you are a new you," you tell yourself, vanquishing your foes and refusing to open the door. Confident, self-assured, and open to new people and experiences, you know these old friends will just have to remain in the background while you reemerge.

Now you hear a sturdy rap, rap, rap. Yay! It's Mr. Wonderful. And you're ready to romp tonight. You open wide the door. Yikes! Something's shadowing his shoulder. You know the all too familiar stance...one shoulder lower than the other. Your new lover is lugging his own luggage—and it's a heavy load.

Undeterred, you welcome him in and offer a drink and some yummy appetizers. He declines. You chat. He sits silently. You turn on the charm. He is cool. There will obviously be three for dinner, and you've only set two places. Not sure of the next step that feminist Erica Jong would advise, you bring up the subject. "Just lay it out there," you tell yourself. "Tell him you're scared, and he's scared."

You thrust your theory on him. He winces as if his appendix needs extracting. Plowing onward, you tell him outright that you too have been afraid of getting involved. He stares and feebly shakes his head, hoping to avoid this headlong collision. Men don't like heavy subjects, and you just laid a brick on his head.

You are now painfully aware that your admission fell on fearful ears. He changes the subject, wolfs down your French cuisine, and makes excuses for an early evening. As he scoots out of his chair, he winces again. "Wow, he spikily states, soothing his shoulder. "I have a little shoulder pain."

You know what that heavy load feels like: tense neck, lower back pain, and sleepless nights. So you smile a caring smile that would make Florence Nightingale proud. "Let's talk when you feel better," you offer. "In the meantime, take care of that shoulder." Yep, this man has baggage, and you can't afford the overage charges. The new you will move on, looking for love and watching for extra suitcases.

Baby Bears Beware

Sipping a second martini with friends, you become acutely aware of the brazen baby bear bellied up to the bar. Obviously tempted by your charms, the cuddly he-cub can't take his eyes off you.

With a sultry but somewhat suspicious smile, you stare at his broad shoulders, his flat stomach, and oh, those protruding pecs. His tee shirt strains to hold back his six-pack abs.

You're no fool. This young lion is on the lookout for an experienced lioness.

Can it really be you, you sexy Siren, who is stimulating this young Adonis? Your trusted therapist's words once more invade your psyche. "If a man is interested in you, don't overthink the situation," she had often stated while soaking up her $250 hourly rate. "Simply smile and slightly stare at him."

You're no fool. This young lion is on the lookout for an experienced lioness. Regardless of his intentions, you determine to let his interest ensue. Whatever you have that he wants, you intend to be generous. Whether you end up with him as a mama bear, sexy seductress, or just a flirty friend, you are going to play this out.

He turns toward your group of gossiping gal pals. Your heart flutters as you question the evolution of your physical prowess over the past few months. "He is looking at me, right?" you pray. "Not the leggy, fish-lipped lioness lingering at the next table?" Your blood pressure spike warns of an impending emergency room visit if this toddler trips over you trying to touch the temptress to your right. Although heart palpitations at your age signal distress, you are willing to defy your doctor for a score with this potential sex slave.

You're in luck tonight. He is walking your way! "Hi, my name is Adam," he says with a smile.

"Oh God," you think. "Can this be

true?" Eve would have nothing on you. You even wish you had sneaked an apple in your bag and could offer him a bite. Tempting this tot is a total turn on. Temporarily channeling your sixties soul sister Mrs. Robinson, you smile and say, "Hello, Jonathan...I mean, Adam."

Uh oh, your mind freezes in a flash. How do you introduce yourself to this neophyte? Do you give your entire divorced name? (No, you refuse to let your ex-husband invade this bliss.) Or do you just give your first name that you detest? "Maybe I should call myself Candy or something that sounds edible," you muse. Rose or Daisy, or something young like Kitty Kat might even induce his interest.

As your lingering wine widows continue wishing for miracles, your very own miracle leans toward you. Their envious eyes betray their wonder at how their mousy friend aroused such a God-child. "Is she emitting a secret scent purchased at Saks?" one ponders while another concludes that you must simply be a silly slut for sending signals to a man half your age.

No matter. You are smitten...and paralyzed...at the same instant. "What if he asks me to dance?" you wonder. Back fat doesn't do well under the pressure of a man's arm during the two-step. And your go-to Dr. Scholl's sandals always tend to shuffle through a samba. Alternate scenarios pummel your thoughts as you continue to contemplate the next move. "Maybe he will ask to drive me home. But how will I secretly send a message to the driver that I'll be skipping the senior bus ride home?" Your most terrifying thought of all is the possibility that he should blurt out, "Let's sleep together." What's a Siren to do in this situation? You suddenly remember your mother warning you to always wear clean underwear when you left the house. Your lagging laundry load demanded that you wear your last clean pair tonight...oops, granny panties.

"Excuse me for staring," baby bear's words interrupt your thoughts as his dimples dare to beam at you, "but you look just like my stepmother's aunt. I couldn't help but ask you your name."

Instant humiliation intrudes on your innards. Slightly nauseous, you wish you hadn't nibbled on so many bar nuts. Trying not to hatefully hiss at the innocent man cub, you set him straight with a smile instead and pivot politely. Disappointed that you'll no longer be robbing the cradle tonight, you willingly lay down your arms before a victorious Mother Nature.

You have to credit your counseling sessions for such a quick recovery. You won't be bitter. Besides, there are plenty of baby bears at this bar. Every Siren knows that older men can present a challenge, and you refuse to resign to false teeth touching your lips, bathroom breaks after every course, and fifty-plus flaccid flesh. "I'm a Siren," you remind yourself and swallow your last sip of martini. "No young thing can resist when I focus." Now it's off to Barnes and Noble for a sexy novel and tomorrow to the facialist to use your Botox discount. A Siren must stay in fine form!

Guys Love Bitches

WHat? Guys love bitchy women? You thought they divorced them for a sweet sex kitten. Wrong! Of all the lessons you've learned so far as a Siren, this may be the most surprising.

A Siren is a woman whom men find irresistible.

A Siren is a woman whom men find irresistible. Consider how Kentucky Derby winners prance with a little savoir-faire. They know they are a prize. In psychology, this is called a self-fulfilling prophecy. If you think you are special (not cocky or conceited), others will think you are special too. Men don't want a mousy mate. They want a prize, not only for them to enjoy but also for their friends to admire. Men are competitive by nature at any age. They don't want last place or anywhere near the bottom rung of the ladder.

Confident women are not clinging vines. They have their own lives with and without their men. You don't cause his cellphone to light up hourly with dreaded demands, "Where are you? And just what are you doing?" Sirens communicate with their men sweetly but succinctly, not in tedious, emotionally laden diatribes. They smile more, babble less, and never forget to ask him his opinion. Men do like to opine. Sirens are efficient and capable, and for all the man knows, the Siren may be straddling a bar stool wooing another helpless chap. Sirens don't divulge every detail.

<hr />

Confident women are not clinging vines. They have their own lives with and without their men.

<hr />

As the Siren displays her independence, Don Juan typically gets more desperate in a quest for control. He may issue repeated compliments, thinking he knows the way to a needy woman's heart. He's talked his way between the sheets many times, but that was before meeting Miss Independent. He's intrigued by her devil may care attitude. When he tells you how ravishing you are, merely say, "Thank you." Never retort, "Oh, not me" or disagree with his assessment. Just affirm his good judgement. Of course, refrain from taking his compliment further by adding self-aggrandizing comments!

Men and money comingle. Men like to take care of a woman, so although you are highly capable, allow your man to spoil you. Thank him sincerely for any surprise, but don't gush. Again, a simple thank you works.

If there are some hateful, misguided malcontents who label a confident, capable, and efficient woman a "bitch," you might appreciate the term, although it's crude and ignorant. Bitchy qualities can make men go crazy to be in your company. They will seek you out and be proud they are your significant other.

Notes from a Siren's Shrink

Another $250, another hour with you bemoaning your relationship status, you stared at the coffee cup your counselor provided. "Trying to find someone is so difficult," you admitted to your analyst. "And I don't want another broken heart."

"Dear God," you thought, "I need sympathy."

"First of all, you must stay in the game," your therapist insisted. "Evading emotional commitments, shunning potential suitors, and avoiding admirers are strategies that are certain to serve you poorly," she conversed convincingly. "Let's spend some time and scrutinize your situation."

You envisioned hundred dollar bills flying from your handbag, landing squarely in your psychologist's purse. To her, "spending time" means you talking, her listening, and the cash register clinking.

"Okay," you meekly agreed.

Surprisingly, she was quite chatty

and serious. Her eye-opening statements shocked you. You've been accustomed to lamenting your station in life and now this mind mender was managing every minute of your session.

"You have to be completely truthful," she said, taking full control of the conversation. "And I," she asserted boldly, "am going to be brutally honest! So here we go."

She teed up the first question. "Do you desire someone who is the same as you are or do you value differences?"

Much of our appeal as women of any age is in effective and appealing communication.

To your surprise, you learn that according to the experts, we do a bit of both. "Finding familiarity with another person makes us feel smart and affirms our judgement," she said. But differences can enhance us by filling in our blanks, she added, noting that a lover's strengths can cover up our weaknesses and vice versa.

"So, what does your intended love creature bring to the party?" she wanted to know about your latest man interest.

"Oh the usual," you thought. "Looks, money, intellect, a fun personality, a support system."

"Don't feel guilty," she soothed. "It's human nature to want something for ourselves. But what can you offer someone else?"

You had to admit you weren't certain of the answer. All you can hear are the screaming blasts from every social media and television image today assuring you that all is lost if you don't hit a 10 on the attractiveness scale. Never mind that your anemic bank account makes you feel doomed to a life of singleness.

"Wrong!" she interrupted your introspection. "Much of our appeal as women of any age is in effective and appealing communication." You already knew that men communicate differently from women. But you were about to receive an eye-opening lesson in Man-Speak 101.

"Let's explore some of the key differences," she said, prompting you to scramble for paper and pen from your purse to take notes. "For example, men like to talk about sports, work, and things." No surprise there. "Women like to talk about relationships and feelings." So, she suggested, in order to bond early in a relationship, women should be well versed in "men talk" and men in "women talk." Women, she added, should keep their stories and explanations short. But men should give more details to a woman. When a man is mad, a woman should try to be quiet and listen. When a woman is angry, the man should risk asking her to tell him more!

Of course, you realized she was speaking in generalities, but you wondered if she was actually on to something. You decided to settle into the couch cushions and make yourself more comfortable.

Women, you learn, are more practical when it comes to life. Men are more idealistic. As your therapist explained that men are not as concerned with a woman's earning power or status as a woman is with a man's, you couldn't help but think of the last loser you'd dismissed when you discovered he sold shoes at the mall. To your surprise, you learn that men take breakups harder than a woman, often blaming themselves. You mentally pictured your exes stuffing their faces with comfort food and smiled. And, your therapist said, women blame the man in a breakup! So true!

It's why some people turn you on and others turn you off.

As you filled your notebook with notations, you marveled at the differences between the sexes.

"When it comes to friends, women value their good friends more than their lover. Men value their mates more than their male friends."

"With few exceptions, women usually desire to go out with men who are interesting and attractive and who carry the potential for a mate. Men want to go out with a woman to have sex!"

"Men think that good sex improves the love quotient, while women think that love improves sex."

Leaving her office that day, your mind was reeling with all this information. Some say there is no such thing as love at first sight, but according to your therapist, that's not so if you believe in it! In fact, she prodded you to be open to finding true love on your next outing, and you willingly took up the challenge.

But first you have to run by the grocery store. While picking up a half-gallon of milk, you spot a handsome man sans a wedding ring standing in the cereal aisle. Before you can turn away, you catch his eye. He smiles. Something inside you reacts and in a very good way. Your therapist warned you this might happen. "Within the first few minutes of meeting your destiny your heart may palpitate and your hands might feel clammy," she said. "You may even feel as if you are on a high."

She was right! Despite aching joints that don't work like they used to, you suddenly feel great. "This is totally psychological," she cautioned. "It is in your brain. Each of us emits smells, looks, sounds, etc. that play with the brains of others. It's why some people turn you on and others turn you off. It has to do with the brain's history—the events and relationships of your past that elicited good responses and others that elicited negative ones."

Whatever is happening to you, you want some more of it please. Can you really induce true love? You're about to find out. In a flash, everything you've learned from all of your counseling sessions comes into play.

"First, to get his attention, flash a big smile." Check.

"Try to meet eyes with him." Done.

"Next, say something. If he says something first, look him in the eye and respond, even if it's something simple."

You slowly and deliberately turn to your potential prince standing in the aisle. "As you get nearer to a prospect, intimacy increases," your therapist's words coax.

"Lightly touch his hand or shoulder." You do so. "Make it brief. Connect with your eyes a little longer after the touch. Be in touch with his body. If he leans toward you, lean toward him. Nod as he speaks, and when he laughs, you laugh." You follow all of the instructions by rote, and it's going well. Very well. You casually make small talk after introducing yourselves.

"Don't be shy or stiff if you like his advances," you hear as your brain recalls your next instruction. "Being coy is not a good trait to exercise in this circumstance. Don't play it cool, as this gets you nowhere. Give him a small compliment and watch his eyes. Are they fixed on you?

Are they wide open or merely slits? Wide pupils mean he is interested. Squinty pupils might help you detect boredom."

"I hope he doesn't think I have macular degeneration," you think, squinting at him as if looking at an Amsler grid. He has wide pupils, you determine. That's good.

Everything seems to be going smoothly, so you follow your therapist's advice and add an element of intimacy. "Tell him a little secret about you," she told you. "Make it something of little significance, but just this one tiny thing will be endearing."

Men love to win the prize.

"Where are you from?" the cereal man wants to know.

You decide to make your response descriptive and deliver the line you've been practicing in the mirror. "I'm from a small town in Ohio that's known for the biggest pumpkin ever grown."

That's perfect. "Give him more than a two-word answer and never disparage your hometown, even if you have to get creative," your therapist had said.

You decide to take it to the next level and agree to go out on a date, but you know to keep it casual and relaxed. You'll be careful not to play hard to get but let him know in a subtle way that you are hard to get when others are concerned.

~~~~~~~~

George Bernard Shaw once said, "Love is the most insane, most delusional, and most transient of passions."

~~~~~~~~

"Men love to win the prize," you tell yourself, repeating what you'd learned in therapy. What your shrink actually advised was, "Let your man give you gifts, but don't appear to be too grateful. Act as though it is totally logical for him to give you gifts and that you are lovable enough to accept them. He will love you more as he will tell himself that he must love you to want to buy things for you." You're thinking way ahead now, but you'll be ready when the time comes.

George Bernard Shaw once said, "Love is the most insane, most delusional, and most transient of passions." And yet you find yourself in good company tonight with thousands upon thousands of single Sirens who want this crazy and fleeting passion anyway and are willing to do everything possible to induce it in a potential suitor. Poets and songwriters have explored love's possibilities and outcomes for centuries. And Sirens have a few decades' experience of their own about a man's soul and psyche and the way to lure him to desire the state of love—both the excitement and the exhaustion of it. You can only hope Mr. Shaw was wrong.

Epilogue

Kiss a Frog

After a horrendous "later in life" divorce, I was thrust into a murky pool of possibilities. To date, or not to date? To try to find love again, or simply give in to late night TV? Would it be TV dinners or candlelight? Dressing up for nights out or frumpy nights alone in fuzzy pjs? The choice was mine.

You may feel that finding a fulfilling relationship is futile. You may even blame your instincts for incredibly poor choices in the past. The worrisome thought that love won't work out for you can do a number on your psyche. "Who could I ever find who would truly love me for 'me'?" you may have wondered.

Siren, it's time to interrogate yourself and recognize that fear and resistance have taken over! Sure, there are some pitfalls in putting yourself out there. The battles of your past have yielded you wins and losses. Only you can know when taking the field again will be worth the cost. Think through the path ahead and ponder the possibilities.

~~~~~~

When you're ready to get back in the game, remember to compete only against yourself.

~~~~~~

When you're ready to get back in the game, remember to compete only against yourself. Let the other cougars, kittens, and female contestants play in their ball court. There are always challengers who will be prettier, smarter, shorter, taller, heavier, or thinner than you are, but battling them to boost your social situation is a recipe for disaster. Competing against yourself, however, assures that you will consistently win because you can always improve yourself. Remember, you can't see what's in front of you if you're looking at your backside!

A life change is a great time to find new friends. So be inclusive. Build your life's tent big enough to shelter others. Everyone loves to be included, and when you do so, it's you who is the biggest winner. When you give new friends and new lovers a new roost, you can bask in the glow of your expanded world. This means finding the positive in others.

It's so easy to be negative and view the good traits of others in ways that make you feel insecure. Other people may require you to turn your head 359 degrees to find something positive, but keep looking. Stretching your neck is good for stress anyway! Listen before you speak. Listening with empathy lessens your need to feel sorry for yourself. You may discover that everyone has challenging times and circumstances. Others may give you new ideas that you are free to use and especially valuable when you give them the credit.

Build your life's tent big enough to shelter others.

Pigeonholes are dark and musty. So open your heart and mind to all kinds of people.

Learn to deal with and accept others' idiosyncrasies, ideas, and ideologies. If one potential suitor doesn't work out, move ahead and keep your eyes wide open. Use a scattergun, not a rifle. Hunting can be fun if there's a wider field of prey!

Siren, you will likely need to kiss a lot of frogs in order to get your prince.

Most important, know that time is not running out. Although frustration and exhaustion can overwhelm you, every Siren's suitor is out there somewhere. You will find him when you finally break free from any negative patterns and are truly ready for love. But, alas, Siren, you will likely need to kiss a lot of frogs in order to get your prince. So, my strongest advice is simply this: kiss, kiss, kiss!

About the Author

Donna has been blessed by her success as a businesswoman, but nothing compares to being married and the proud mother of two Southern gentlemen, Brandon and Collin, who love their families and are successful in their own right.

She has extensive experience in the classroom and the boardroom, earning her BSE and MSE in Counseling from Midwestern State University, as well as completing the Harvard Business School OPM Management Program. Donna has served as a mayor and leader in local city government and continues to serve the greater Dallas community she loves in a variety of civic and cultural roles.

However, it's the lessons Donna has learned in the school of life that she most wants to share with others. *Cinderella Has Cellulite* is Donna's first book, followed by *Born to Build: How Dallas Became a Shopper's Paradise* and *Sex and the Siren*. Her writing has previously been published as a columnist for *The News and Times*,

Tri-Cities, owned by *The Dallas Morning News.* As a frequent public speaker, she enjoys making others laugh and opening their eyes to a new perspective on some of life's most challenging experiences.

She married her husband, Herb, in 2012 and they enjoy traveling together and spending time with family and friends. Herb and Donna live in Dallas, Texas.

Printed in Great Britain
by Amazon